# FOOD

## SILLY SCIENCE FOR SMART KIDS

Written by

**Robin Twiddy**

Designed &
illustrated by

**Amy Li**

# BookLife
## PUBLISHING

©2020
**BookLife Publishing Ltd.**
**King's Lynn**
**Norfolk, PE30 4LS**

ISBN: 978-1-78637-998-6

**Written by:**
Robin Twiddy

**Edited by:**
Madeline Tyler

**Designed by:**
Amy Li

A catalogue record for this book is available from the British Library.

**PHOTO CREDITS:** Images are courtesy of Shutterstock.com.
With thanks to Getty Images, Thinkstock Photo and iStockPhoto.
Cover: Curly Pat, Recurring Images: bosotochka (header font), Sonechko57 (blobs), Anna Frajtova, Volha Shaulkavets (food/cutlery vectors), Visual Generation (lab vector background), Amy Li (additional illustrations). P2–3 – Brent Hofacker, p4–5 – Christiana Mustion, Dmitry Kalinovsky, Elnur, Victor Moussa, Visual Generation, Volha Shaukavets, p6–7 – Georgios Kollidas, Elnur, Visual Generation, Ines Behrens-Kunkel, Nastia Gomanova, p8–9 – Christian Lagerek, Mountain Brothers, nathigai, svtdesign, tratong, Tartila, p10–11 – nutua, Kolesov Sergei, Valentyn Volkov, GoodStudio, studiovin, Anastasiia Kozubenko, p12–13 – Studio Romantic, Gregory Johnston, chainarong06, Lucky clover, Sapann Design, Artisticco, p14–15 – Africa Studio, Visual Generation, Aaron Amat, adike, Jezper, Artit Fongfung AF, Elnur, serazetdinov, p16–17 – Earch, leungchopan, Tanya Sid, TheVisualsYouNeed, Grimgram, p18–19 – megaflop, Mything, Stocklifemax, VikiVector, zcw, p20–21 – Aaron Amat, Happy cake Happy café, MriMan, tynyuk, MatoomMi, Shirstok, Mara008, p22–23 – pikepicture, CuteCute, cameilia, baibaz, Zastolskiy Victor, KatyGr5, p24–25 – Fancy Tapis, Africa Studio, Roi and Roi, nekoztudio, Syda Productions, Bk87, StockVector, p26–27 – teekayu, Mazur Travel, mayakova, NotionPic, Borjaika, p28–29 – Anna Violet, Andrew Rybalko, Rachata Teyparsit Nawamin, Ganis

# CONTENTS

Words that look like **THIS** are explained in the glossary on page 31.

# SCIENCE:

## Why So Serious?

We all know science, don't we? Boring people in boring white coats, writing boring things on boring clipboards. Boring, boring, boring, right? Wrong! What if I told you that science can be sillier than you have ever imagined?

*I am very serious!*

*Sniff, sniff... That's a five on the Fart Intensity Scale.*

## Silly FOOD

Imagine rows of scientists experimenting to find out how slippery a banana peel really is. Does that seem serious to you? Scientists find ways to measure the world around us and the things that appear in nature. There is even a scientist who created a way to measure how smelly a fart is!

# Welcome to the SILLY ZONE

You are about to enter the Silly Zone. In this book you will find scientists doing the strangest things. Get ready!

I don't think that hat would taste any better if I closed my eyes.

## Real SCIENCE

Although this science all seems very silly, there is often a very good reason behind it all, or at least something very useful that we can learn from it. Some scientists found that the smell and taste of food can be changed by its appearance. From that, we have learnt that taste isn't just in the mouth – it is in the mind too!

# Running on CUSTARD

## Would YOU Choose Right?

Picture yourself being chased by angry crocodiles. Scary, right? Now imagine that the only escape is either through thick jungle or across a lake of custard. What do you do? The correct answer is to run across the custard, assuming that you can keep running until you reach the other side.

## Non-Newtonian LIQUIDS

That's right, you can run on custard! But how? Custard is a non-Newtonian liquid. This means that it is a liquid that doesn't behave like other liquids normally do. Sometimes it acts like a liquid but sometimes it acts like a solid.

What do you mean custard doesn't follow my law of **VISCOSITY**?

I shouldn't have punched that custard. I thought it was going to be soft.

# WHY Don't I Understand Custard?

Custard usually acts like a liquid, but when it is impacted (that means hit or struck), it behaves like a solid. Newtonian fluids, such as water, only change their **PROPERTIES** with temperature and **PRESSURE**. Non-Newtonian fluids are immediately changed by the **FORCES** acting on them at that moment.

## Swimming POOL of Custard

In one experiment, a man tried to walk across a swimming pool filled with custard. When he stood still, he sunk slowly into the custard. He needed to run or walk quickly to make the custard act like a solid so that it could hold him up.

But he did it! He walked on custard.

# POTATO

## People on Planes

### How MANY Potatoes?

Boeing, a company that makes aeroplanes, spends a surprising amount of money on potatoes. But why? What could potatoes have to do with planes? They didn't buy 9,000 kilograms of potatoes for their lunches.

One potato, two potato...

### WHY (-Fi) Potatoes?

If you entered a Boeing plane when they were testing Wi-Fi signals, you would be greeted by rows and rows of seats filled with potatoes. This is science! This is silly science! This is silly spud science! So, what is going on here?

Where is that Wi-Fi signal? I need to finish downloading Edward Potato Hands.

# Potato
# PE★OPLE

There is a very good reason that all those seats are filled with spuds. Surprisingly, potatoes affect Wi-Fi signals in a very similar way to how people's bodies do. Filling the plane with 'potato people' allows the engineers to work out where the Wi-Fi signals are strongest and weakest and how bodies change those signals.

Wi-Fi was invented in 1979 and uses **RADIO WAVES**.

## Why N★T People?

Of course, the engineers at Boeing would get more accurate information from filling the plane with people, but potatoes are better than people in some ways. Firstly, potatoes are cheaper than people, and secondly, potatoes never get bored!

Try reading the dictionary to a potato. It won't get bored. Potatoes never get bored.

9

# How to STACK Watermelons

## Don't PANIC

Don't worry, it's been solved. The biggest problem to face humankind: how to stack watermelons! For millennia – no, since the dawn of time itself – people in supermarkets have been placing watermelons on top of each other just to see them all roll away under tables and out of arm's reach. But no more!

That was a beautiful pyramid five minutes ago. Science, help!

## HOW Did They Do It?

You won't believe this, but it wasn't done by **CROSSBREEDING** plants, or changing the watermelon on a **GENETIC** level. No, they were grown in a box. When the watermelon is very small, a glass box is placed around it. When the melon gets bigger, it grows into the shape of the box.

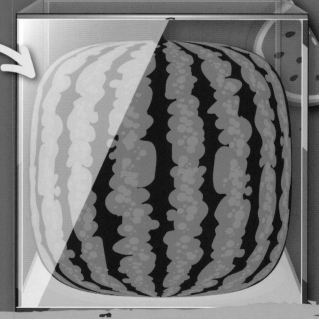

The glass allows sunlight to reach the watermelon. This is important to make sure that it grows.

# WHY

## Did They Do It?

The square watermelon was invented in Japan. Surprisingly, people in Japan had more than one reason for inventing and embracing the square watermelon. Firstly, they are easier to stack and transport, but more importantly they fit better into small Japanese fridge freezers.

Some of these designer watermelons cost as much as £20,000.

# SQUARES

## Aren't Good Enough?

But squares are rubbish. Nobody wants a square watermelon anymore. They are just so boring. How about a heart-shaped watermelon, or maybe a pyramid-shaped watermelon? These are all real watermelons that you can really buy!

What's next, round watermelons?

# Becoming a Champion Speed EATER

> So, you want to be the best? The very best there ever was? Eating more than the rest? Well, speed is the test, if you want to be the best!

Speed eaters are people who eat food very quickly competitively. This means that they try to eat more food than their opponents in a quicker time.

Where do all the hot dogs go?

## Science STUDIES the Body of a Speed Eater

Scientists compared a professional speed eater to a person with a normal, healthy appetite to see what was different. Each of them had 12 minutes to eat as many hot dogs as they could. The very serious scientists noticed some very strange things.

# What Is Happening INSIDE a Speed Eater?

An ordinary human stomach contracts when you eat something. This means that it squeezes together. It does this to help break up food for **DIGESTION**. However, the stomach of the speed eater didn't contract – it just kept stretching.

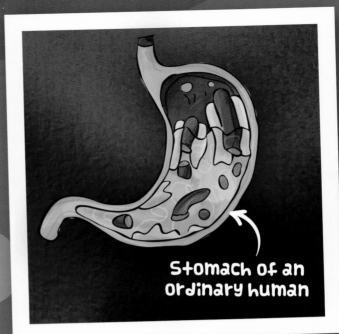

Stomach of an ordinary human

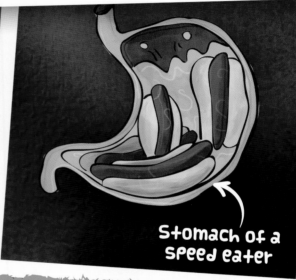

Stomach of a speed eater

See how a speed eater's stomach stretches.

Health Warning: Speed eating often leads to some serious health issues in later life!

## Big  Small?

What is the best body type for speed eating? Big? Small? Muscly? A surprising number of competitive speed eaters are skinny. The reason that thin people are sometimes better at speed eating is that their stomachs can stretch without much fat getting in the way.

Thanks, science!

13

# PEANUT
## Butter Is Forever

## Something, Something, PORRIDGE

It can be hard to concentrate when you are sandwich... Wait no, I mean hungry. Food keeps sneaking into your thoughts and then, before you know it, you are writing 'crisps' into every sentence. These scientists were studying diamonds when it seems they got distracted by thoughts about peanut butter.

Please, I am so hungry. Just a little peanut butter, please!

Scientists spent a lot of money turning peanut butter into diamonds in their lab. It is very impressive, but it does seem a little bit silly. Making diamonds this way is too expensive for them to be used in jewellery, and besides, nobody wants a chocolate and diamond sandwich!

# WHAT Are They Doing?

The experiments recreated the conditions deep underground, where extreme pressure and extreme heat can change the very nature of a thing, such as peanut butter. Diamonds are made from **ATOMS** of **CARBON** arranged in a particular way. Peanut butter also contains a surprising amount of carbon.

+ Heat
+ Pressure
:

# But WHY?

As always, there are some surprisingly useful things we have learnt from this very silly science. The scientists behind the experiment believe that it has given them a better understanding of how the planet was formed billions of years ago.

Was the world made of peanut butter?

No, the world wasn't made of peanut butter!

# WASABI

## Smoke Alarmy

## SMELL You Later

Have you ever got something spicy in your eyes or up your nose? It is pretty hard to ignore. Scientists received an award for designing and testing a new type of smoke alarm that fills the area with the strong smell of wasabi.

## WHAT is Wasabi?

Wasabi is a thick, green root that grows in Japan. It is used to make a spicy powder or paste that is usually added to fish. The same **CHEMICAL** that gives it its kick is found in mustard and horseradish.

# Just the RIGHT Amount...

In tests, the scientists found that the wasabi smoke alarm woke sleeping people in under three minutes. But it took a lot of tests to get the right balance of wasabi so that it would wake people up without hurting their eyes or noses!

Just sign this and go to sleep.

**CONTRACT**

I will allow scientists to spray chemicals in my face while I am asleep.

SIGNED...................

# But WHY?

Although this seems silly, or more like a practical joke than real science, there is a real need for a smoke alarm like this. For people who are deaf or hard of hearing, this alarm could save their life. Traditional smoke alarms make a sound that is hard to ignore for many people, but this one makes a smell that is hard to ignore.

Just don't burn the wasabi!

# Why Is My WEE Green and Smelly?

## The SNIFF Test

Two scientists stand in front of a cup of wee. The first picks it up, sniffs it, then sets it back down. "Interesting," she says. The next scientist picks it up and does the same. Then they start on the next cup of wee. Scientists are very silly sometimes.

## ASPARAGUS: Wee Transformer

What were those scientists doing? For most people, eating asparagus produces a very strange side effect. Their wee becomes really smelly, and some people even find that their wee turns green.

# Can't SMELL the wee

Some people claim that their wee doesn't smell any different after eating asparagus. Science is about asking the big questions – the questions nobody else is asking. Does their wee not smell? Or can they not smell the asparagus wee?

What if you eat a whole bundle of asparagus?

Nope, I can't smell a thing!

# The RESULTS
## From the Wee Test

After smelling lots of cups of wee, the scientists decided that, while some people do not make smelly wee when they eat asparagus, most people who report not smelling it do actually have wee that smells – they just can't smell it, even in others.

This science was definitely silly, but did we learn anything useful? Probably not.

# Brain FREEZE

## The MYSTERY of Brain Freeze

For years, nobody really knew what caused brain freeze. Well, we knew that it happened when you ate or drank something cold or dived into cold water, but we didn't know what it was. Well, again, we knew it was a headache caused by cold things. But why? What was happening inside the head?

Quick, get the scientists. We need to get to the bottom of this.

## STUDYING Brain Freeze

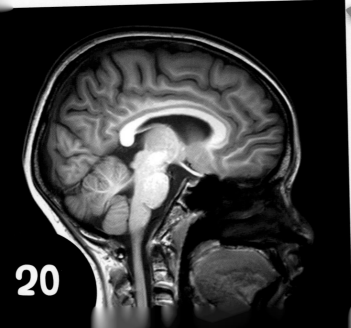

The scientists gave people brain freeze by making them drink cold water through a straw pointed at the roof of their mouths. At the same time, they used an **ULTRASOUND** to see what was happening inside people's heads when they had brain freeze.

# The ULTRASOUND

So, what did they find? When people reported having brain freeze, the scientists could see that there was more blood flowing to the brain. The blood was flowing through an artery that sits in the brain behind the eyes.

## CRUEL
### or Clever?

It is not clear if this science can help people. All we really know for sure is that these scientists spent a few days giving other people headaches. Do we have a cure for brain freeze? No.

# IS the CHILLI a Lie?

## Can't Take the HEAT

Have you eaten a chilli before? Isn't it funny that it is hot even when it is cold! When we say that our mouths are on fire when eating spicy food, we mean it! It really does feel like our mouths are on fire and science has found out why.

## How do we TASTE?

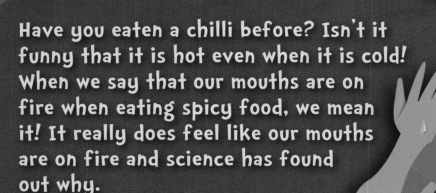

I hope you don't know how human beings taste! No, we are looking at how we know what food tastes like. Our mouths are very clever; when you put food in your mouth, it tells your brain whether the food is sour, sweet, salty, bitter or **UMAMI**, and if it is hot or cold.

Yuck! It's horrible, don't eat that again!

Tongues do a lot of the taste work.

# Heat is NOT a Taste

When we eat 'hot' food, such as chillies, we experience heat in our mouths. That is not a taste, it is actually pain. A chemical called capsaicin in spicy food tricks the tongue into thinking that it is hot. It activates the same nerves that tell our brains about the temperature of food.

You are feeling very hot!

# THANKS, Science

Science has taught us that what we experience isn't always real. This sensation of heat is actually an illusion, like a magician on a stage who makes us believe that he has sawn someone in half!

# WHAT Can't Potatoes Do?

Spuds, taters, jackets, king of the crisps, pre-chips... Whatever you want to call them, potatoes are pretty special. Here are some of the special things they do.

## Potato POWER

People have known that you can power a light bulb with a potato for a while, but science has now shown that boiling a potato for eight minutes will make it produce ten times the amount of power. Imagine a future with potato-powered homes!

## Rust-Removing TATERS

Rust is really hard to remove, unless you have a potato! Simply add a bit of salt, baking soda or washing up soap to your potato, then get rubbing. The oxalic acid in the potato will break down the rust. Thank you, science, and thank you, potato!

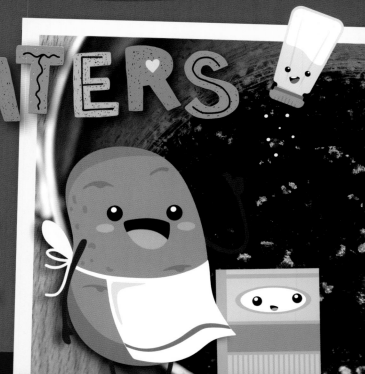

I will be back in three potatoes, Dad!

# TIME
## of the Potato

In ancient Peru, the Inca people loved potatoes. Potatoes were so important that the Inca measured time by how long it took a potato to cook!

# PLASTIC
## Alternative

Can the potato help save the planet? Plastic is a real problem and is causing serious pollution problems because it doesn't **BIODEGRADE**.
Enter the potato. Very clever scientists have found a way to use potatoes to make things such as knives, forks and straws. These would be much better for the planet.

Thank you, Super Potato!

# POO  Coffee

## ADULTS
### Are Weird

Lots of adults love coffee, even though it is bitter and hot, and really smelly. But do you know what the most expensive coffee is? It's a coffee made with coffee beans that have already been eaten and then pooed out by a big cat-like creature!

What are you looking at me like that for?

Civets aren't actually cats, but they are very similar.

## The SCIENCE Behind Poo Coffee

A scientist claimed that the coffee berries chosen by the civet are better and that the animal's digestion helps start a chemical reaction called **FERMENTATION** that improves the flavour. Well, you can't argue with logic like that.

# POO INSPECTOR

This type of coffee has created an entirely new job: the civet poo inspector. If the science is correct, then the best coffee beans will be found in the poo of wild civets. Someone has to hunt for that poo and find the beans in it.

# WHY IS It SO Expensive?

These silly scientists started a whole **INDUSTRY** from their research into poo found in the jungle. It just goes to show that it is all in how you look at it. Some people see poo where a silly scientist sees something to make a drink from.

It's made HOW?!

# Secret Science of Smelly FARTS

## WHAT Is a Fart?

They can be loud or silent, very smelly or just a little pungent, but importantly, they can be described scientifically! Farts are usually made up of nitrogen, hydrogen, a bit of carbon dioxide, some methane and a little oxygen. Farts are the escaping gases our stomachs make when they digest food. Different food makes different farts!

I must get to the bottom of this!

## The GREAT Fart Detector

Believe it or not, a fart detector has been invented. It is made up of a hydrogen sulphide monitor, a thermometer and a microphone. Beware, secret farter, you cannot hide in the crowd anymore.

# MEASURING Farts

Fart testing lab

The fart detector measures three elements of a fart: stench, temperature and sound. Using a computer, the detector **RANKS** these elements: how smelly, how hot and how loud it was. It then provides a ranking from one to nine.

It is smelly, it is unpleasant, but most of all, it is deeply funny.

## Surprising USES of a Fart Detector

The fart detector is definitely silly science at its finest, but it has real-world uses. There is interest from vets to use it to check the health of farm animals. It turns out that you can tell a lot about the health of cows from the quality of their farts.

What are you going to do with that?

# FOOD:
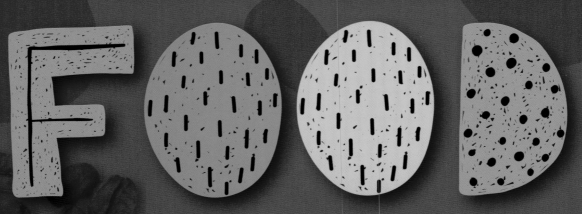
## Glorious or Gross?

Who knew that scientists were so silly?! Smelling wee, detecting farts, hunting for poo and tasting hot food, all in the name of science. Even the cafeteria isn't safe from them... Keep an eye out in your school for sneaky scientists testing puddings and stealing all the custard!

Food is just another thing that science has made silly and gross. So, don't forget the next time you are eating a potato, that science has proven it is the best food. Thank you, science, and stay silly!

# GLOSSARY

**atoms**  the basic units making up chemical elements such as oxygen or hydrogen

**biodegrade**  to break down because of natural living things, such as bacteria

**carbon**  a chemical element that is found in all living things and can be found in diamonds in its purest form

**chemical**  a substance that materials are made from

**crossbreeding**  when two or more different types of plant are made to breed together to make new types of plants with features from each plant

**digestion**  the breaking down of food in the stomach so that the body can absorb what it needs

**fermentation**  the process in which sugar changes into alcohol, producing bubbles of gas

**forces**  invisible energies that push, pull or move objects

**genetic**  to do with genes, which are instructions passed on from a parent to their offspring that help decide characteristics such as eye colour

**industry**  the activity of turning raw materials into products

**pressure**  a continuous physical force that acts on an object, which is caused by something pressing against it

**properties**  physical qualities of a material

**radio waves**  waves of energy that can be used to send information to machines over long distances

**ranks**  places things in order of value or importance, such as from worst to best

**ultrasound**  a type of medical scan that shows what is happening inside the body using sound waves

**umami**  one of the five basic tastes — foods that have a strong umami taste include soy sauce, mushrooms and tomatoes

**viscosity**  the qualities of a liquid, how it rests and how it flows

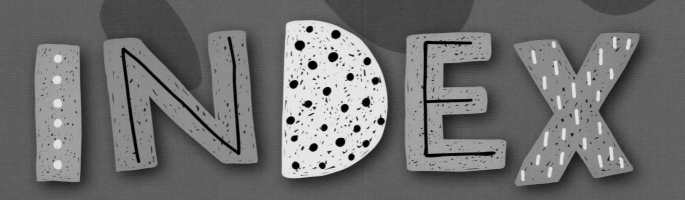

# INDEX